Head Lines

Poems and Provocations

Will Schmit

Head Lines

Copyright © 2020 -© 2019 by Will Schmit

All rights reserved. No part of this publication may be reproduced or transmitted in any form or by any electronic or mechanical means including photo copying, recording, or any information storage and retrieval system now known or to be invented, without permission in writing from the publisher or the author.

Publisher's Cataloging-in-Publication data
Name: Will Schmit
Title: Head Lines: Subtitle: Poems and Provocations/by Will Schmit
Identifiers: LCCN:
ISBN: 978-1-952369-01-8 Revised Edition
Subjects: 1. Poetry/Subjects & Themes/Inspirational & Religious
2. Religion/Spirituality
3. Religion/Christian Living/Spiritual Growth

Cover art : Dennis Henry Schmit
Illustrations: Dave O'Connell
Author photo: Justin Grimaldo, Sight Seer Productions

Published by EA Books Publishing
a division of
Living Parables of Central Florida, Inc. a 501c3

EABooksPublishing.com

"Will's poetry is Maya Angelou meets
Tom Waits in the Psalms ...
Transcendent!

— Bryan Duncan, DOVE Award winning
Recording Artist & Song Writer

Also by Will Schmit

Jesus Inside: A Prison Minister's Memoir and Training Manual

Published by EA Books Publishing

Bring to Glory
a recording of spoken word with music
produced by Russ Paladino, Very Cool Media, Inc.

Both are available at www.schmitbooks.com

DEDICATION

Jesus is the Author and Perfecter of my faith, all recent developments of my poetic perspective are a result of my forever union with my bride Trey.

CONTENTS

ACKNOWLEDGMENTS	10
PREFACE	11
New Rule	1
Celestial Sandbox	2
String Together	3
Tide Fool	4
Unsung Song	5
Thumbs Up	6
Hydro Low	7
Pilgrim	8
String of Lights	9
Moccasin	10
One Nation Under	12
Song Bark	14
Knee Stain	15
Teeth of God	16
Flowers and Arrows	17
Well Healed	19
Baby Blanket	20
Cusp Overflows	21
Water Lines	23
Sound Bites the Hand	24
Little Star	26
New Listing	28
Word Play	30

Egg Hunt	31
Mud Pi	32
Coltrane's Rain	33
Wet Whistle	34
Sewing Lesson	35
From Dust Where We Played	36
Color Wheel	37
News In New Light	38
The Regular	39
Love is in the Air We Breathe	40
Parade	42
Tweet Street	43
Wipe Away	44
Bee My Neighbor	45
Push then Pull	46
Basilica Blues	47
Tree Mend Us	49
Front Row	50
Shopping Heart	52
Pelican Bay Lights	54
Our Neighborhood Now	56
Be of Good Chirp	58
The Face in The Vase	59
God Footing	60
Passing Lane	61
Sabbath	62
Miriam Too	63

Place Setting	64
House of Miracles	65
Live Longhand and Prosper	66
Prodigal Pop	67
Now You See Me	68
Stefano's Pick	70
Fall Back	71
The Hat has Fits	72
Spring Clinging	74
Wood You	75
Write Brothers	76
Showtime	77
Lap of the Lord	78
Jesus in Jeans	82
Choir Practice	84
Hit Send	86

ACKNOWLEDGMENTS

Phonetically it has been argued the most beautiful words in the English language are 'cellar door', but what can ever sound sweeter to our ears than 'thank you'? Please allow me to thank my first readers for giving me a second chance. Russ Paladino, Aaron Green, Neil Montgomery, Bill Garfield, Olivia Farr, your willingness to peruse my lines encourages me to trust the process.

PREFACE

Writing poetry is a process of tapping found jewels into the crowns of the passerby. These intuitive arrangements of words serve to align our souls with reflective purpose. I have been writing, publishing, and performing poetry for fifty years. I like to think I know what I'm doing, occasionally I can prove it. My hope is you'll find inspiration in these pages and begin to gather your own handful of gems from the stones we sometimes find in our shoes.

Head Lines

New Rule

You are what you hear;
bottle nosed whale slide blues,
mint and fern whipping the air,

to turn your head
the voice of the Shepherd
whistling through His teeth.

Facts and faith, a jumble
of Scrabble letters face down,
we use to spell ourselves.

It's possible to have the Christ
in ways unbelievable to believers,
but to believe He has us,
that's worth breaking bread.

Celestial Sandbox

A stand-alone God,
not alone,
caws us to sing.

Music in orbits,
hearts beat
the point pounded home.

Life in light years,
mothers
close as stars apart.

Celestial tryouts boom
behind planets,
a child in the sand box,
croons.

String Together

A string of naked ladies,
the pink flower,
face away the ridge road.

Orange sunset spent
on the odd nude
stalks.

The ocean, not a mile away,
but the hill, parched.

Our blankets catch shooting stars,
nameless streaks
scorch the night.

Their Father, our Father, knows them,
but for us it's just point at heaven
and awe.

Tide Fool

What I read,
hand shading the gold glint
of the ocean,
is my scribbled pocket book
of hope.

A smooth cold rock
turns in my hand, like the chorus
of a secret sacred song.

The bench I watch the west from
is a pew to the wide sky and white caps.

What I negotiate here, what I navigate,
what I need is a way to walk on land,
as well as He traversed the waves.

Unsung Song

You know that time of morning
when the fog begins to lift,
you see your breath trail streaming
and you know that it's a gift.

Once constant pains and worries
are loose paddles in the drift,
early birds and nightingales
toss Charlie Parker riffs.

When we hear of someone's passing,
into the great beyond,
and wish we could tell them
that their life will carry on,

our heartbeat keeps repeating
not believing they are gone,
a signal uncompleted
unsure notes to start a song.

Thumbs Up

Angels hitchhike
on the truck side of lonely.
Lovely weeds bend in the flying dust
of wheels stopping to start again.

The driver might chatter football,
the radio Gospel, or tripe.
This part of the Damascus road
is between homes, jobs, baths.

The Son of Man
has nowhere the lay His head.
Transients, the easy victims
of innocence and dumpster diseases.

The next Samaritan binds
the next wounds.
Our daily bread buttered,
one side at a time.

Hydro Low

Water and worry leak
to the lowest level,
a fool's pool
spiraling the spirit
to depths
beneath the necessary steps.

It takes hydro-logic
to lift water
higher than clouded despair.
To rise as steam,
we admit wet
as requisite.

Our Engineer's faith;
part bending knee,
part pouring cups
to the least of these,
cuts across current fashion,
chiding the waves to be still.

There is living water
and there is a stagnant well.
One can't flow forward
by going back.
The well-worn path is reasonable,
but making sense of resistance, is a mist.

Pilgrim

What we learned
can be forgot,
what we know
dismissed.

Who we are
is debatable,
why we're here
the cosmic question.

Whom we love,
and who loves us, is
the suring thing,
the truth we bring to
table.

String of Lights

The wren wonders at outdoor
Christmas lights,
not much there for nesting,
the wires make poor worms,
the bulbs, sharp white on green leaves,
confuse with slight shadows
and heat.

To a bird's eye, this
seven dollar string of electric
adornment, is supernatural, and to us,
on this holiday of heaven come to earth,
the Light of the World hanging from eaves
and roof gutters, sparkles in the eyes
of the children His birth makes us all.

Angels and doves top
the indoor trees, visitors
and families, all wise,
bask in glowing hearts, the Gift
of never ending love swaddle wrapped,
waiting,
like Santa's cookies on a plate, to be shared.

Moccasin

Mowed the lawn in moccasins
to make a point about January
being different in the great
and generous Northwest.

My Daddy, frostbit, from chopping ice
off the walk a few decades
and states east of here, would marvel
at anything so green close to his birthday.

Late in life, we might miss
the things our children notice,
like an upstart of daffodils closer
to the curb than the wild.

The shut down mower and smell of simple labor
whispers what God thought
when He said, "Well that's enough mountains,
for now."

One long path of soft steps,
makes everything we climb,
puny.

One Nation Under

If it dehumanizes, it's propaganda. If it takes an isolated incident and makes a general statement, it's propaganda. If it aims to convince you that most people, if not everybody, feels or thinks like you, it's propaganda. If it aims to convince you that most people, if not everybody, that is not like you is against you, it's propaganda. If it offers outrage as solace, it's propaganda. If it insists isolation is a deeper connection, it's propaganda. If it keeps you on edge, instead of on your knees, it's propaganda.

1 John 4 encourages us to weigh things spiritually. "Beloved, do not believe every spirit, but test the spirits, whether they are of God; because many false prophets have gone out into the world."

Amazingly enough John had this insight long before Facebook gave us a barrage of opposing viewpoints at the click of a mouse. Propaganda, according to Webster's, is the methodical spread of ideas or information to injure a movement, cause, nation, or a people group. It is maliciousness designed, and disguised, for profit. Media based on misinformation is a sleight of hand trick masking the iron fist of crowd control in a velvet glove.

John says in verse 17 of chapter 4, "Love has been perfected among us in this: that we may have boldness in the day of judgment; because as He is, so are we in this world. There is no fear in love: but perfect love casts out fear, because fear involves torment. He who fears has not been made perfect in love. We love Him, because He first loved us. If someone says, "I love God" and yet hates his brother, he is a liar; for he who does not love his brother whom he has seen, how can he love God whom he has not seen? And this command we have from Him: that he who loves God must love his brother also."

Love is not a stage prop. It is serious, and delightful. It is rigorous. It comforts. It confounds our real enemy. Love gives identity by sharing dignity with all of us made in God's image. Love advances, when the temptation arises to retreat into our preferred political camp, the Gospel intervenes. Mark 9:47 "Whoever receives one of these little children in My Name, receives Me; and whoever receives Me, receives Him Who sent Me."

These little children, in God's eyes, are whomever we wish to ignore, denigrate, or despise. They could be Muslims, Methodists, Mexicans, or our fellow Americans. Despite all the rhetoric and rabble rousing, every person in our path is an opportunity to realize grace. If we truly wish to make America great, let's enlist the words of Jesus Who admonishes us to become servants of all.

Song Bark

Wintered leaves rattle
at apple branch end,
the lone music makers
in the life of the tree.

A delayed rendezvous
gives me glimpse
of a natural chorus
ignored.

Jesus said, "The very stones
will cry out…"

Bus stop arbor
doing its best.

Knee Stain

Drops swell at branch tip
to catch bubble light and, glass like,
wink to the waiting grass.

Even with scrubbing
the new dirt of the strawberry hill
paves the crease in my finger skin.

Between pig pen, and prodigal proof,
I garden with the angel of Eden,
hoping to keep a foot in the gate.

Put down roots, pull up weeds
hoping for another hand
on the wheelbarrow.

Father and Son team,
such a threat to the devil,
such a joy in the spring wet mud.

Teeth of God

(for Frank)

I clipped blue iris,
those little teeth of God,
the day your grandson died.

Like spears in a vase
the cut stems still
take water.

The window light,
filtered by glass,
frames life.

Two weeks on the planet,
we're too weak, to stand
alone.

A breath suspended, family upended, tend
to the flowers, then the tears.

Flowers and Arrows

William wore a hair shirt
somewhere around Italy,
shows you what I know about saints.

Little picture cards litter
the chaplain's desk,
flowers and arrows pierce the heart.

A yard and B yard assemblies,
melting pot of hot heads
and maimed spirits.

We gather to pray here,
two or more
the math of heaven.

Just a closer walk;
the forgiven getting up,
time after time, doing time.

We leave one chair open
for who went before,
and who comes after.

Each lost sheep
makes a sound only
the Shepherd can hear.

Well Healed

I wear a dead chef's boots
to preach in prison.

Black Johnny Cash jeans
because clichés don't clash
with the dress code.

I speak no Spanish, recognize
no tattoos, never slept behind bars.

I'm welcome because I show up,
shake hands, pray, and come back.

Familiar equals family
when everything is strained and chained.

The insiders know my heart is locked with theirs,
clanging echoes drive me home.

Baby Blanket

The dream fogs forward.
We're weeks away
from grand baby to be,
plums barely clinging to the branch.

The ocean, a little further than
the next door rooster, breaks on the beach
morning after morning, anticipating footsteps
as our family strolls.

The math of compassion adding up,
the little ones make us larger.
Passing down humor, songs,
and curls, decades away from going grey.

God has no grandchildren, the one thing
we can pity. The smallest finger
He'll ever feel in His hand
is ours.

Cusp Overflows

She caught the last of summer
by the sleeve, granddaughter born
two days before the Fall change.

Easy to predict strawberries
and melons, both parents are gardeners,
the dirt will turn up.

Newest human I ever met
forty five minutes in,
pounds, ounces, inches, stretch our hearts.

The light in her eyes
lights the room. Lighting
the world, starts tomorrow.

Water Lines

Raindrops connect us to the clouds,
sometimes in whisper, sometimes
in a bullhorn from the balcony,
getting wet is getting the message.

Like love, at the border of a family,
there's enough to go around,
we stand in it, faces up,
hands outstretched like pails and a chalice.

It's up there, what we need down here.
Balloons, kites, and prayers know this;
the falling down, the coming to terms
with the simple miracle of our blue planet.

Wet back, dry throat,
the clouds migrate across oceans of sand.
A cup of water to the least of these
is grace breaking open the damned.

Sound Bites the Hand

Chamomile yellows low to the shifting
ground, another boot is keeping toes
from knowing what grows below.

The rain is washing a child's blood.
The sun wasting time on fresh graves.
The wind is way ahead of soundless music.

Sirens, bulletins, bullets;
new vocabulary words
at the kindergarten.

Smiling through scars,
shared meals prepare
to heal survivors.

Families break bread,
stones break windows.
Poems break into silence.

Little Star

Abandoned shopping cart
in a creek,
twinkle twinkle.

Rainy season; plastic tarps
rumble in the wind, blankets
become roofs.

Our homegrown homeless get
headlines when cops clear
the campground.

The war they're running from
is quieter than Syria,
the battlefield of what if…

Away in a manger,
a motel for the night,

any question where He'd be born
again this Christmas?

New Listing

A young friend of mine's best friend from high school died a few days ago from an apparent overdose. It wasn't an accident. Suicide. Young twenties. Relationship difficulties complicated his early re-hab progress. The enemy came but to lie, steal, and destroy. Jesus came that we may have life more abundantly, but as the poet John Donne says, "Any man's death diminishes"... us all.

My friend cried while telling me how horrible he felt not being able to watch his friend use heroin and now wondering what, if anything, he might have done to help the young man get sober. The second guessing afterthought is an all too common pain. I held him and told him to feel everything and raise his kids. I doubt there is a modern family among us that doesn't have some version of this story line cutting to the bone. Addiction is not fiction, but it is not the truth of who we are meant to be.

I'm clean twenty plus years, lots of people are, and more and more of us need to be. When I was using I couldn't imagine a day without getting loaded. What fun would that be? How could I feel special, unique, clever, connected, etc unless I was high? I went to meetings. I met people who knew my insides better than I did. I put the drugs down and began a process of not putting people down to make myself feel taller. It is a practice we could all use more of, especially where we might intersect the fragile.

Life and death is in the power of the tongue. Telling someone you love them helps them believe it. Of course actions speak louder than words, but words are the bullets and bandages in the battle of the mind. Tell someone you love them today. Tell yourself. Tell me.

Jesus loves you, I love you, and the list goes on and on and on from there. Make sure you add a few more names, could be the best thing you do today and tomorrow.

Word Play

Just by changing a letter
greed becomes green.
Imagine such a world
whispering.

The power of words
starts with smaller things;
hen scratches,
the marks on a tortoise back.

The hand, writing,
is stopped from all other work,
the pot left to simmer as thoughts do
in a burst of clouds.

The Word became flesh.
We return the favor, spelling
with sticks in the sand,
between the wash of waves.

Egg Hunt

Awake,
a grave refuses
permanence.

Wide eyed lily
scent
to a blind world.

Now the Blood spilled
is the Blood welling up
in forgiveness.

Spared despair, we color eggs
in a bowl and wait,
as our not-a-ghost Guest

takes
another minute
to wash the family's feet.

Mud Pi

Thrill my eyes with mud fresh path,
tree fallen,
daffodil known to slug banana
and branch light golden.

Spear my ears with surf pound, new
creek gargle and cormorant squawk.

Let my feet find mint folds
and flat beach when the rocks spill.

Lungs suck spray gulls play shadow wheels
between fish gulps.

My desk abandoned,
phone face dark,
nearer my God to Thee
not more possible.

but still,

the effort to love,

easier,

with breeze.

Coltrane's Rain

This perfecting night the stars
fit between each branch
of the fruiting plum.

The yard, mowed or un-mowed,
greenly slopes toward the ocean
below the moon.

The wet sodden air
seeks our skin as we rush inside
like water, from the sudden rain.

We credit butterflies with kisses,
but it's all the world blowing us
His love song supreme.

Wet Whistle

Where I go to hear
from God
is not necessarily nearer,
the dark wood in my hand just a spoon
stained from stirring coffee,
the stars pulsing as I adjust my eyes.

Where I go
to hear from God
is closer to the voices in my heart
than head, and although not a fan of horses,
I sense them beating truth around the bend.

Where I go to hear from God
plumbs the creek cold water, quick trickle,
a droplet, running wrist to elbow, tickling,
reflects the ocean as His smiling tears.

Sewing Lesson

Blackbirds leave the wire
like so many needles abandoning
the seam.

We're undone under
sniper laden skies,
a broken tale of light lacking direction.

I can't get nearer my God to Thee
unless I get closer to you,
and you, and you, to me.

Hate is the shortest four-letter word,
love, the invisible,
takes its place in line.

From Dust Where We Played

Look onto the sky
as dust rises to make music
of rainbows, and the things
water brings
before the sun.

Grace spins in spontaneous space,
the fingertip of His creation. We
don't hear what hasn't yet been played,
but it is written; every breath,
from the mouth of God,
is a song.

Color Wheel

The new road
to the old moon
follows a line of wild hickories
and neon pizza lights.

A roadside cascade of tumbling tomatoes
splits its sides laughing
at chip paint billboards
promising a future home.

Shaded bricks bounce the top
of the pictured cul de sac
like a juggler's ball
in the hand of a one armed dancer.

Everything in the sky
has wings and a song. Listening,
down here, is a type of flight.
Hope is for rainbows behind the storm.

News In New Light

The un-neighborly dog
barked til three,
my dog, calm as a cow,
slept, one leg on,
one leg off the pillow.

The news was already bad by midnight,
dawn just made it harder to swallow.
God doesn't strike me as a tip-toeing Father,
he graces every despot with resistance.

The commonsense of the sun,
the compassion of the wind,
will steal the thunder of hard blowing coal fire.
Cool water will yet have its day.

Eye for an eye technology
can't see the forest shrinking,
eye to eye theology
blinks at the unsettling light.

The Regular

The chip in the mug
lets my lip know the sipping side.
Burnt beans and water mark
the morning begun.

Just out of daybreak's glare,
we prop on pillows and psalms,
choosing once and future dreams
to share before chores.

You can call Love what you want,
I know what fills my cup spills
into a smile.

Love is in the Air We Breathe

Somehow becoming a climate crisis denier has become the social and political equivalent of defending God's sovereign power. The world He asks us not to be of isn't the earth, the natural vulnerable planet we are to steward, but the corrupt world of men's lust for power. Trying to excuse, or ignore, the consequences of our environmental choices because we believe God could fix it all in a snap is lazy theology. Be ye transformed, by the renewal of your energy, is a gospel all of creation is groaning to hear.

Wisdom applied to our household trash, our consumption habits, and our modes of transportation would be a welcome change of scenery. Just by changing a letter, greed becomes green. What responsible personal choices might we make today, and tomorrow, to insure future todays and tomorrows for our grandkids and their grandkids?

There is nothing sacred about polluting our air and water. To do so for the profit of a few at the expense of the many is oppression. Our faith is built upon doing for the least of these and the least we can do is save a little breathing space for future use. The Tree of Life is any oxygen producing plant converting the CO_2 gas in the air from a poison to a positive. I'd love to see a church youth group planting real live oaks, in righteousness, in the hood.

Picking up trash at the beach, giving carpool rides to shut-ins, pulling a neighbor's weeds, by hand, to eliminate the use of carcinogenic herbicide are all community service projects waiting for the armies of the Lord to volunteer. Walt Kelly, creator of Pogo, a syndicated comic strip of yesteryear quipped, "We have met the enemy and he is us." It is true the battle is the Lord's, but like the Marines, He is looking for good personnel.

The song says they will know we are Christians by our love. Wouldn't it be lovely if they knew us by our carbon footprint as well?

Parade

Day works into night,
a great blue heron silhouettes black against
the last pink slip of sunset.

Near the end of my route,
kitchen lights outnumber the stars,
the year's new twilight shadows me home.

If nothing had changed, this dusk, would be
no different, but our flag snaps
in bitter gusts of assumption.

Now a planet blinks through the trees.
Stern branches, still bare, bow in a promise
of bud, leaf, and flower.

Hope will spring eternal,
because the Eternal rises from mud,
and pours, like rain, into the street.

Tweet Street

It is the other
in your brother
that makes the hood interesting.

Spices from the window,
music in the air,
all the names of God in dialects.

What the missing fathers miss
we are to fill in,
whole hearts hold attention.

Walk a mile, search
door to door.
Orphans, of all ages, want you home.

Wipe Away

The storm is a ways away,
maybe a mile or more.
The first drops dot the window
then stream, in tears, as they have for days.
The grey roil hints at a darker day,
and the wind suggests the straightest trees
have a weakness. The wet soaks in, leaks out,
even the promise of flowers loses color.

The silver lining,
in the smile of an umbrella, is child's play.
The adult version wearies, works, and wonders
when the waiting ends.
Prayer is a rain boot.
What comes from the ground,
in spring, reminds us, at the Resurrection,
there won't be a dry eye in the house.

Bee My Neighbor

Flowers never dream of what people do.
Even taking water in a vase,
if there's light, they face it.

"Consider," He said. Colorful
instruction looms
in a bloom.

Follow the bees, neighbor.
Share the sweet promised land
of unbordered honey.

Push then Pull

The romance
of collecting life in a cardboard
house by the river is getting damp
today.

June clouds
June rains,
June bugs.

The towering stack of aluminum
cans might bring beer money,
or canned beans,
if the fire stays lit.

I'm observing the speed limit,
hustling by,
but not much else.

Can't bear to look
at what only God sees.

Basilica Blues

If we lost all marble columns,
Venetian mosaics,
and blue vaulted basilicas,
would the sky be canvas enough
to hold our hearts still?

The Church, not a building
but building our steps.
One foot, lighted by the Lamp,
in front of the other,
waiting for the Gold Winged Lion
to whisper, or roar.

St. Mark's Piazza Venice 2017

Tree Mend Us

Our soles know the forest best.
Redwood heights lift our eyes.
We smell the ancient barks
and branches, hear centuries of birds,
but it's the ground, the matted
leaf, needle, and root
that pads the path
calling us home.

In the cathedral
of long shadowed trunks
we unlikely priests press
the weight of the next step.
As part of the dance,
the panorama smiles
at what God sees
in the climbing pilgrim.

Front Row

No one follows the unsung.
The rut in the road
was cut
by the wheels of change.

Maybe one chair in the room
squirms at the lie,
whispers in the hall,
alerts the ear.

And then, two, or more,
gathered together
like found coins,
add value to conviction.

Maybe it's Congress,
maybe it's church,
the truth only sets you free
as you speak.

Shopping Heart
(for Bob Goff)

Tuesdays I drive into town with Jesus.
We don't talk much. He gives me
His "What more needs to be said" look
and fiddles with the radio to get pysched.

We pour love at the Walmart,
walking down the aisles like they were water.
Sometimes folks raise their hand
halfway to their face as if they recognize Him
in each other.

There's little else to go on,
gentle, humble in heart.
Mercy, how He teases me
to let Him drive.

Pelican Bay Lights

I beat the sun to your town,
watched the surf light grey the beach
before the cardboard kings begin
sorting treasures in humped blanket rolls.

The prison's here. The one with
the sign, not some mental
restriction, or emotional
underbelly in revolt.

Guards, entry cards, bars,
inside, inmates await
family visits, mail call,
court dates and answered prayers.

My cowboy boots click
the corridors, state issued ID
swinging like Jesus on a stick
from my neck.

Volunteer chaplain
fitted for a vest, meant
to deter violence
while preaching Peace.

Every day is Easter
walking, like Lazarus,
from cell block
to a concrete chapel.

Angels hover
as fluorescent lights flicker.
The piano's out of tune,
even in Spanish.

The brothers sit
while I stand in the gap.
Our Father
lends His Son.

The hum of a hymn,
the comfort of a known page
turning, the ritual of handshakes,
kneeling.

All that is holy
is here, all that is evil,
available upon request,
same as everywhere.

Came to serve,
we get our game, our name
from Him. Play and pray
'til the whistle blows.

The ride home, alone
but not, a chance to whisper
through the trees and live, like roots,
underground.

Our Neighborhood Now

I knelt, silently, with a world of believers in Saint Peter's Basilica. The colors of skin, the shapes of faces, the cut of the wardrobe all part of the fabric weaving us together. The pilgrimage, long a tradition, made new by the escape from irrational politics to a place of faith. 'Set your mind on things above' is a tad easier when the ceiling vaults to a sky like proportion, the prayers of centuries past echoing just beyond candlelit whispers.

The devout, come out of the crowd, take a knee, and return to the turning world. What we bring to the throne comes home with us, an adopted dove of peace forever ours to feed and keep. We are connected by the presence of Spirit seeking an indwelling relationship. This brotherhood, this kinship sealed in the Lord's Prayer. Our Father, emphasis on Our, welcomes us with robes and rings.

We run from love to find Love running to us bright as a train leaving a lifelong tunnel. The mind clears, the soul quickens, the heart expands, it really is our neighbor as ourselves that defines our legacy, our children's inheritance. We are all immigrants to the citizenship of heaven. It is not our home, but His. He invites us to take it by the hand by lending a hand to those in need. This is the custom of being heavenly. Grace is best known in movement, in generosity, in compassionate care, in extended family. Our Father.

The language of worship doesn't need to be spoken, or translated. Adoration is the door we enter to know His people. While we are yet still afar off, while we are yet sinners, we are known, called home, and called to reconcile. Faith without action is dead. The most simple thing to share is the light in our eyes, and the greatest thing to receive is His perspective.

I went to church in a foreign land with Egyptians, Romanians, Italians, Germans, and a host of others. The whole time I had a sense of God opening his photo album to show me how His children have grown. Everywhere we turn, there is God with His Selfie-stick saying, "Smile."

Be of Good Chirp

The branch at bud point,
lightly bears the warbler's weight,
shakes free of frost,
and offers a blossom peek
to the sun.

Winter's run it's damp course,
the blue that matters most
reclaims the sky, the song,
the long awaited chirp,
and twitter, rules the air.

I've seen this sixty times or so,
the promise held, the crocus
smile, the smell of roots
and ambitious dirt
turning the earth vibrant.

Spring forward, back
to life, a calendar theme.
Resurrection palatable,
plausible, yet
extreme.

The worm's eye view
tells us more.
There's truth below ground
the clouds envy.
He is risen, in deed.

The Face in The Vase

The final splay of our tulip,
table top Ferris wheel
petals purple wide
as a lion's mane.

Flowering jumble
in a water jar, the bulb
bringing life and the stem
snipped for a day's bouquet.

The kitchen wild for it,
the meal graced,
the wet grey spring
proposes at the window.

Husband and wife,
working the odd hours,
chance a glance at the bloom
and remember Who gives.

God Footing

Dancing feet
Write with bones
Each pound
In the ground
Is a letter of intent.

The jump
Pumps the heart
Drumming
The earth's ear
To attention

Wings sing
Above arms in flight
The spread of influence
Flexes muscled
Memory

Pray the unsilent
Witness speaks
To your hands
As fists unfold
To grasp this.

Passing Lane

The Trinity River rippled silver
under the charred rocks
of last season's fires.
Needle thin pine spines
silhouette the ridge,
crows ignore the highway to cross
the valley.

We climb the mountain, in the slow lane,
then glide, inland, toward the heat.
Our conversion turns as slow as asphalt allows,
we break to hear the stream's quick splash
become a sun warmed prayer
for progress.

The cathedral of the wild,
road angels dip the running water
to baptize travelers in the sight
of Shasta's snows.
Our pilgrimage gains a thousand feet,
a thousand wings.

Sabbath

From the sink
I open the window to you,
the flower picker. Red handled
scissors grasping green grace
as you top the spent poppies
at the edge of the garden bathed in light,
color, and the late August sun.

Sunday's tradition bakes
on a bare arm, cups of red tea
hold the last sip for good measure,
the folding chairs, as if from Solomon's
tent, speak of wisdom's triumph
over gravity and the genius of a cat
seeking shade.

Troubles make their own fence,
the gate hanging like a dog's tongue,
the song of the sky is yet another blues,
the tintinnabular voice of humming
alarms going silent.

The rest is easy.
Trust, the blankest page in the book,
waits for a pen, that waits for a hand,
that waits for God,
Who waits, like the rest of us, for the weekend.

Miriam Too

Blame slurs the moon,
stutters the birds,
unties the string of things.

The woman in the square,
rocks at the ready
in the hands of power.

One finger in the wind
writing in the dirt,
"Love you", neighbor.

The scene plays out,
daughter after daughter,
begging to be believed.

The first stone,
a brick through the window,
a burning cross.

What we lay down
as life, as law,
deflects the Light.

Place Setting

Geese line flying
low under a half moon,
copper sun paving
the west road.
I'm hours, a lifetime,
from Your side of the street,
perspective, a weather vane
on a wind-blown barn.

Safe, in Your arms,
is the smoke choked heart,
the waiting table set in reflective glass.
Cold water pours from the ocean
on the burning forest
of daughters known and
daughters lost,
a son's boots sort the path.

An afternoon star claims
the early dark of the season,
branches prepare to bare
the burden of calling life.
Unless the squeal of children
echoes our prayer,
any vote of confidence
is just a road sign, torn.

House of Miracles

The house of miracles
grew up around us.
The green leaf curtains
crawled up the fog bright windows
like dancing lace,
the swinging lantern
issued stars, fireflies, and
sparks of insight.

The house of miracles grew up
around us. The gravy boat
poured everyday like Thanksgiving.
Our mirror reflected smiles.
I was so surprised my key
still fit the lock, all my shirts
had buttons and the toaster had five settings
for, "Yes, Please."

It was only a time ago
we were quarreling,
questioning.
Then the two year old began to sing
and our ears went straight up
to the sky.

Live Longhand and Prosper
(for Rudy)

I tuck all my fear
in an envelope,
fold it in my back pocket,
and wait in line to post it.

It's unsolicited,
this blue note.
An apology,
the rarest of terms.

Jockeying for sympathy
passes for conversation,
so, unsigned, I send paper
to hold your perspective.

As you smooth the crease,
you might notice
the page is waiting
for reply.

Moving a pen
is how we chart and change
our mind. The words, spell
themselves.

The same size
as a grocery list,
the lines just as short,
a poem reads our future.

Prodigal Pop

A curtain of birds
slights the silver bay light.
July vines vault the hedge
with berry blossoms and thorns.

Our son's back to work, and
my coffee's warm as the sun.
I'll seek counsel
to deal with happy.

A timely God
is all we ask,
an eternal smile
is how He answers.

This parenting thing
covers the world,
uncovers the heart,
discovers the real.

My father would say,
"So soon old,
so late smart."
The walk sign is flashing
at the crossroads of joy.

Now You See Me

The invisible look at things differently. They see themselves comfortable in their dining room chair, before the abduction, the deportation. They see their bed made and waiting for a safe sleep. Routine and normal, these things become miraculous when stolen.

Missing people used to be an other-worldly problem, maybe it made some twisted sense in the Third World, but not in our neighborhood. Milk carton photos of missing children, Amber Alerts, newsreels of ICE agents kicking in doors, missionaries returning home with stories of fighting sex traffickers, the new normal has breached the realm of the unimaginable. The Old Testament laments of captive Israel in Babylon are being played out right down the street.

Jesus says in Matthew 12:30, "He who is not with Me is against Me, he who does not gather with Me, scatters abroad." It is the conclusion of His 'a house divided against itself cannot stand' admonishment. Divide and conquer has always been our enemy's first line of attack. Separated from God's intent by the serpent the garden dwellers become refugees in a hostile territory. Dividing our church politically, racially, or economically belies Christ's assertion the Kingdom of God is at hand.

The undesirable, the undeserving, the forgotten, the forlorn, the captive, the banished, this is us. In faith, hope, and charity there is no them. Those who prey upon the weak dismiss our thoughts and prayers. In Jesus' time suggesting that a Samaritan could be good was an almost impossible stretch of the imagination, a bit like conservatives or liberals today putting the shoe on the other foot. It was the Samaritan's action of going out of his way to care for a victim of society that made the story stick.

The outreach Jesus advocates isn't a demographic pack the pews on Sunday strategy as much as it is extending our hand, the one with the Kingdom in it, to help. He calls us friend. It's an honor, a privilege, and a call to action. Insuring each other's personal safety is the compassionate component of the gift of salvation. The Lord sets a banquet for us in the face of our enemy, it is our place to make sure the vulnerable are seated at the table.

Stefano's Pick

The good fig
provides pride, shade,
 and fruit.

The family bicycle glides
under a branch,
to rest.

Whether the day is done,
or just begun,
the tree houses the thrush.

At the corner lot,
a reminder,
of Paradise.

Fall Back

Since the darkness all I see
is tunnels.

Long buried things
bearing hatchets.

The stars are sparks
of a larger black,
immune to bullets.

What pulses,
one hand in front of the other,
is the street, waiting to cross, with the Light.

The Hat has Fits

The problem with romance
is spelling. Horizon too pretty to reach,
too constant to ignore.

Stars cast their shadow
on the wandering soul,
home soil just a boot print.

Lonely whispers
ain't the only sound
in the clouds.

When God wants to get away
He picks a lonely man
to walk it out.

The curve of a river
indicates
He thought about it.

There is a people
searching for repair
to damaged wings.

Settle down
is not a phrase
a mountain speaks.

Naming the beasts
is the first part
of a long song.

When she sings back
the coyotes mute,
for the cowboy's echo.

Spring Clinging

Spent cherry blossoms
slip heavenly downward
to the Sunday lawn, un-mowed.

Slight air streams bend their path,
generations of poets ride each petal
to the ground.

As greed burns the earth,
and smoke chokes our hearts,
the lady bug's warning is just a polka-dot
shell.

The future's stinging eyes
read our apologies
in fury.

We trusted God, until He said,
"Be careful!"

Wood You

Lake
rest your eyes, blue
green lapping wavelet,
kayak paddle drip song,
gathered sons and sun stretch
the heron flight.

Inland
heat treats the bones,
hope floats on the rolling wake
of tolerant fishermen,
as we walkabouts wear relief
instead of sleeves.

Angling oaks
thread water edged pines
to tickle the forever sky.
When the hushed church
seeks, the creek
instructs.

Write Brothers

The write feather
in the wind
twirls
on the head of a pin.

The forest sees
through us,
branch light as owls,
dark as a horse.

Takes a big foot
to mark the way
we should go
to water.

The pages here,
heavy as rooted stones,
turn graves into benches,
as is custom.

When the song
breaks from the sky,
sunbeams spell
relief for the wintered.

The Invisible smiles
at every visit,
stirs the fire
in our heart.

Showtime

My horn's in a hard case
in case my heart hears news.
The handle holds together,
tape and worn glue,
my Maestro moved to Europe
without a word, just a blue
note.

For some years, decades,
I unpack alone, feign guiding
tones, bend the air around
midnight and whisper shadows
to light, remember the ring
in the bell and the soft reed
rasping.

How my hands hold the push
and sway is a story loose
from the page, an age of chairs
facing the music, yes,
and the never known crowd
he walked through
to chord the stage.

The melancholy is only
one world, the holy
another chorus altogether.
The concrete room I play
holds and releases prisoners.
The Echo bows and smiles
for the missing.

Lap of the Lord

I lay my head in the lap
Of the Lord.
The wrinkled clay of my brow
smoothed by His thumb.
In my hair His breeze
is a blue blanket to my soul.
His sunlight warm silk to my face.
The weight of my worries
gives way to prayer,
the problems of my bones
absolve in song.
The bricks around my heart
become berries,
to spread on toast,
All the sins of my tongue, every boast,
insult, and lie, melt into broth and butter.

I lay my head
In the lap of the Lord.
My eyes trace the Hand
that moves the stars,
my ears echo with the brook voice
breaking over stones.
My toes are glad in clover.
Let me vow to walk every corner I've cut
again. Heel to toe, straight and narrow.
Arise in me, Dear God, with the artistry
to repaint every wall I've beat my head against.

I'm hungry now for the soup
I cried in. Let me blow
on the spoon of grace You give us,
bow my head and dip my bread.
Amen.

Jesus in Jeans

(for Cindy)

Jesus in jeans
isn't much of a stretch,
a tool belt, thermos,
some decent boots.
He might shave for Sunday,
sit in the back of pew
of every church in the world
and smile at the preacher.

He's an everyday Savior these days,
raising our spirits,
raising our sights.
Story is He overheard a café conversation,
"O halfway houses are alright, I guess
but not on my street."
Jesus leaned in,
paid for the gentleman's coffee,
and whispered, "According to My Father
the whole world's a halfway house.
Don't forget to tip the waitress."

He's an everyday Savior these days,
donating blood again.
Every time we lift a finger to help
we're helped.
What would Jesus do
without us? Truth is
He couldn't stand it,
that's why He stands at the door,
ready to knock some sense of Him
into the heart of the world.

Choir Practice

(for Pastor Lorie)

A constant constellation,
The Worthy Star
watches the lonely.

The night, silent again,
throbs in stellar concert.
Midnight, clear.

Shepherds await returning angels,
tell us when and where
to stand.

The wind moves as one
dark song, searching
for singers.

A slender thread stitches
silver bells,
heart by heart, by heart.

Hit Send

David, King of Israel, but do we have his crown in a museum? No. Mighty warrior, but is his slingshot on display for all posterity? No, again. His musical abilities were renown throughout the land, but his harp hangs not on any wall. What we have of this soul, this beloved of God, is his poetry, his psalms.

As a poet myself I am impressed, amazed, and grateful that David's cries to the Source of the skies are still resounding. His encounters with the Lord still ring true generations later in every cultural context around our sun circling globe. Whether the accepted translation says, "The Lord is my Shepherd, I shall not want," or, "The Lord is my Mighty Herdsman, and I am as firm as a spear in the ground," the personal sense of being cared for by the Almighty is tangible, terrific, and true.

His inquiring lyrics sprang from a combination of longing and belonging. Because we have this condition, this opportunity, in common I wonder if we miss out on a degree of intimacy when we recite David's lines in lieu of writing our own. Might not the cries of our times prove to be eternal enough to encourage the future? Surely, He who made the ear is listening with that in mind.

A modern psalm ought to be a calming balm from the assurance Jesus gives us that nothing can snatch us from the palm of His Hand. We are held, in awe, by the One we hold in awe. No matter if our mumblings sound like baby talk to us, to Our Father, like any new and forever parent, it becomes the song of ages. Get out your pencil, or crayon, and try it. Jot something down and then, lift it up. Maybe it starts out something like, "I lay my head in the Lap of the Lord…"

www.ingramcontent.com/pod-product-compliance
Lightning Source LLC
Chambersburg PA
CBHW022012120526
44592CB00034B/788